GREAT BALLS OF DOUBT

Great Balls
of Doubt

POEMS AND PROSE POEMS

Mark Terrill

ILLUSTRATED BY
Jon Langford

Verse Chorus Press

Published in 2020 by Verse Chorus Press, Portland, Oregon | versechorus.com
Front cover art: "In the Shark Bar," by Jon Langford
Cover and book design by Steve Connell | steveconnell.net

Grateful acknowledgments are due to the editors and publishers of the following chapbooks, broadsides, journals, and anthologies, in print and online, in which some of these pieces, or versions thereof, first appeared: *Bareknuckle Poet, Bateau, Blades, Bloodroot, Blue Book, BODY, The Café Review, Change Remains Suspended* (Feral Press, 2013), *Cloudbank, Columbia Poetry Review, Competitive Decadence* (New Feral Press, 2017), *Cutthroat, Diagram, Diamonds & Sapience* (Dark Style, 2017), *Down at the Gate* (Feral Press, 2013), *Empty Mirror, Fact-Simile, The French Literary Review, Hanging Loose, Heavy Bear, Knockout, Laughing Butcher Berlin Blues* (Poetry Salzburg, 2010), *Little Horse's Magazine, Louis Liard, The Meadow, Milk, Molly Bloom, New Madrid, NOON: journal of the short poem, Oranges & Sardines, Otata, Other Rooms, Poetry Salzburg Review, Red Mountain Review, Retort Magazine, The Salvador-Dalai-Lama Express* (Mainstreet Rag, 2009), *Sand, Section 8, Superabundance* (Longhouse, 2008), *Turntable & Blue Light, Up All Night* (Longhouse, 2011), *Upstairs at Duroc, U.S. 1 Worksheets, Water~Stone Review* and *Zoland Poetry*. "A Pair of Darts" appeared in *A Pair of Darts*, a limited edition chapbook published by Feral Press. "A Poem for Radios" appeared as a mini-broadside in the *Equinox Tinysides* collection, published by Fact-Simile Editions. "The Wheel" and "A Poem for Blondi" originally appeared as a broadsheet published by Kater Murr's Press. "The Art of Victory" appeared in *Bukowski Anthology* from Silver Birch Press. "A Poem for the Rear Guard" appeared in *Apocalypse Anthology*, published by Flying Guillotine Press. Some of these poems appeared in *Postcard from Mount Sumeru*, in the Chapbook of the Quarter series published by Bottle of Smoke Press. "Interzone" and "Out-the-Window Poems" both appeared as broadsides published by Bottle of Smoke Press. "A Poem for Heroes" was performed and recorded by the Enablers for their album *Blown Realms and Stalled Explosions* (Exile on Mainstream / Lancashire and Somerset, 2011).

Country of manufacture as stated on the last page of this book

Library of Congress Cataloging-in-Publication Data

Names: Terrill, Mark, author. | Langford, Jon, 1957- illustrator.
Title: Great balls of doubt : poems and prose poems / Mark Terrill ;
    illustrated by Jon Langford.
Description: First edition. | Portland, Oregon : Verse Chorus Press, 2020.
    | Summary: "A collection of 96 recent poems and prose poems, with 25
    illustrations by Jon Langford"-- Provided by publisher.
Identifiers: LCCN 2019037876 | ISBN 9781891241666 (paperback)
Subjects: LCGFT: Poetry.
Classification: LCC PS3620.E765 G74 2020 | DDC 811/.6--dc23
LC record available at https://lccn.loc.gov/2019037876

CONTENTS

DOWN AT THE GATE

You could never add up
all the years it took
for this time to finally come.

Soldiers down at the gate,
smoking, teasing the dogs,
telling politically incorrect jokes,

index fingers poised
on the polished trigger guards
of government issue rifles.

A harvest moon hangs back
in the branches of the cottonwoods
that will soon be felled.

Cigarettes form arcs of orange light
suggesting battle plans
and the shape of a woman's hips.

One soldier's peeing in the mailbox,
another is hatching a plan
for what to do with the cat.

They're going to protect you,
or they're going to kill you,
it really doesn't matter anymore.

THE VERGE

That woman with the white hair
in the red coat
on the green bike
pedaling along the canal
against October's blaze of colors—

Did she just emerge
from some Van Gogh painting
or is she on the verge
of heading back into one
and taking me with her?

WAITING FOR PERNOD

Walking up the rue d'Odessa
then walking back down again
it's tough to contemplate
the parameters of transcendence
when you're looking for a bar

a bar in which a woman once
whispered something into your ear
a bar in which Beckett once
waited interminably for the barman
to bring him a glass of Pernod.

On the boulevard Edgar-Quinet
your shadow suddenly detaches
disappears into a film noir alley
leaving you in Sartre's onerous ontology
like a hapless fly in a chunk of amber.

In the café some are seated
others are getting up and going away
some with a feisty truculence some
with a wavering kind of hesitation
that distends the definition of time

while others are trying to appropriate
the shambling remains of your subjectivity.
And in the many stately plane trees
on the other side of the square
the red squirrels are dying of old age.

A POEM FOR BLONDI

Inside the tangled coils of history
the coordinates of right and wrong
are hot and sticky
and a little confused
and the orphic static slaps back
like a dark song by Brecht
echoing from some fluorescent-lit
shadowless white laundry room
far beyond Munich boulevards,
the hacksaw blade of the Alps
and distant Berchtesgaden,
where a few grainy minutes
of spliced-in footage show
failed-art-student vegetarian
non-smoker Adolf Hitler
cuddling with beloved Blondi
on the sun-raked terrace,
his faithful German shepherd
who later served her country
by testing the cyanide pills
in the bunker in Berlin
proving that they functioned
perfectly well indeed
and thus opening up the way
to the way beyond.

A POEM FOR METROPOLITANS

Some people were killing some other people in a very brutal and inhuman way. You could watch it on television and it was "real" but you couldn't do anything about it. The pictures were tiring and I switched off the set and went out into the streets, well aware of the "mood" I was in, which, despite the immediate circumstances, was one of vague euphoria, brought on no doubt by the spectacular dynamics of my metropolitan surroundings. I went into my favorite restaurant just off the square and had my favorite meal. I went into my favorite café on the boulevard and had my favorite coffee. I went into my favorite bar in the narrow alley and drank many of my favorite drinks, one after the other. I went into my favorite brothel down by the harbor and made it with my favorite whore, again and again. When I got back home I saw that the same people were still killing the same people in the very same brutal and inhuman way, again and again. No one was learning anything and the story was getting old fast. It seemed like the oldest show in the world and it wasn't even a show. I switched off the set and turned my attention to the stove. I rattled the grate and watched the sparking coals drop down into the ash box. It seemed like the oldest show in the world and it wasn't even a show.

A POEM FOR PHILOSOPHERS

Some old proto-Freudian out of the German yellow pages is looking up at me from the kitchen floor where he's installing a new P-trap under the kitchen sink, telling me about how things are and how they used to be and the glaring differences between the two. What is it about these German plumbers who invariably turn the slightest incident into a philosophical conundrum?

Beclouded in my grid of craziness and conceit, the months go stuttering by with their recondite equanimity. For all these years now I've been hardening on the outside, softening on the inside, my soul a flimsy exoskeleton oxidizing in the exhaust fumes, now alarmingly transparent in the harsh light of day. I wouldn't so much mind the long fall from grace if it didn't have to last for an entire lifetime.

RIMBAUD RELOADED

"Je est un autre."—Arthur Rimbaud

Boot heels scuffing on
red-light district cobblestones
on my way down to the harbor of Hamburg
where cranes and containers
oblique light and Rothko colors abound.

If I is another then who am I?
Or must we devise some Cartesian qualifier
like "I is another, therefore I am"?
Or is it just the objective "I" versus
the subjective "I" and may the best "I" win?

And is that a pistachio-hued vintage
Mercedes 290 SL hardtop-convertible pimpmobile
generously trimmed with gleaming chrome
parked in front of that bordello
that I'm pretty sure is Polish—

or must all such speculations
constantly be born into something called language
and a splenetic stream
of continuous interior dialogue
between one self and another?

THE FALL COLLECTION

What the morning has to say to you in its violent October language—the riot of red and orange and yellow, the anarchy of a splash of pink—all that blue and green and brown—you have to step back a bit to take it all in—you need to unfurl the law of Knowing and Unknowing to find out where you really stand. Then the memory thing kicks in—a flashback cutaway all the way back to a time before the time you call now—a red Dodge pickup coated in road grime, a gallon jug of tequila finished off in a rusty boxcar—bad new friends and a menacing turquoise and silver ring decorating a dirty clenched fist hovering right there in your face—but all those years have left you on your own to conjecture in a clime of unmade decisions and forfeited wisdom in which neither stratagems of creation nor some skeletal romance can save you now. The way an artist leads the light into a painting—that process reversed—is the only way out of this world.

"A PAIR OF DARTS"

That's the gauche English translation
of "Un par de banderillas,"
the caption on the back of the
Spanish bullfight postcard,
as though it were a pub sport
and not a blood sport,
as though the bull on the flipside
would just get a few minus points
for having four pairs of harpoon-tipped
70-centimeter wooden shafts
decorated with brightly colored ruffles
rammed into his blood-sopped neck,
as though by having Gertrude Stein
and Alice B. Toklas sitting in the
wooden barreras in the ring at Valencia
to see Joselito and his brother
long before they waxed enthusiastic
to the yet-to-be-aficionado Hemingway
it might put death in the afternoon
into the innocuous light of an
existential parlor game
played with a pair of darts
and a few tender buttons.

TERRA NOVA

Down another road
the latitudes give way
to something as plain
as place.

To live in that hotel
and clink glasses nightly
with the old cronies
in the bar downstairs . . .

The small victories
and the great defeats compound daily
and the cast-iron pen nib
weighs a ton

scratching across the paper
leaving its little river of ink
behind to dry
in the freshening breeze

coming in off the Pacific Ocean
where empty-handed conquistadors
once turned around in the fog
and sailed for home.

THE TIME BEFORE TIME

Parked in line, red light, waiting at the ferry slip,
towering twin cement grain silos gilded
in angled rays of late afternoon sun,

an entire lifetime shudders by
in the few ticking minutes
it takes to think about it.

In the time before time
a memory persists
of no solitary entity by itself.

If, like Einstein said, light bends,
then time must bend with it.
Thus the dubious return of what once went forth.

The bright light of uncertainty;
the less certain you are, the brighter it gets,
until all is blinding light.

Some things are what they appear to be;
others are not. The light turns green.
Departure is imminent.

IN THE SHARK BAR

First the old ways, then the new ways, then the old ways again. Seen through the rain-spattered windows of the Haifisch Bar in Hamburg a gigantic container ship passes by, moving slowly down the Elbe in blustering winds, slanting rain and the glinting lights of the spectrally nocturnal harbor.

Imagery on that kind of scale invariably behooves a rigorously metaphorical point of view—but you're not watching shadows on the back wall of Plato's cave and it's in your bloodstream that the unspoken words will never win the long war of attrition between faith and reason, between absence and presence.

The jukebox stops and Roxy Music's over-the-top post-modern pop resonates in the air like an invisible sonic cloud for a few splintered moments before the white-haired bartender dressed like the Man in Black reaches for his battered acoustic guitar from its place behind the bar. First the old ways, then the new ways, then the old ways again.

THE ALLEGORY OF TIME

The broken mirror above the cracked sink
in the cheap hotel room in the ancient harbor
on the other side of the island
seems to be saying all there is to be said
about the passing of time
and all that passes with it
except that the language of things
is always spoken in ideas
which—unlike reality—are finite in nature
and destined to implode and disappear
when the thinker stops thinking—
like a dying star in a collapsing galaxy
at the other end of the universe
the light of which could never possibly
reach us in time.

NOVEMBER POEM

A distance with a mountain in it.
A tree
with five yellow leaves;
one for each season and one
for the mind.

Inauspicious saturnine attitudes
as autumn gives way to winter,
funerals give way to births—
the demiurge working in
intransigently cyclic ways.

The one—countered by the other—
this end of the desk sagging under
its burden of books & papers—
the other end an empty see-saw seat
rising up toward the clouds.

All the conversations into which
I did not enter today—
with my neighbors, my wife, my self—
all those words not made redundant—
like money in the bank.

MEMO FROM SIDDHARTHA

If you can navigate the subway station in Hamburg-Altona climb the stairs and walk through the train station among the infinite flux of faces and figures in that arbitrary barrage of citizens rushing through the early-morning hustle and bustle and come out on the other side still feeling good about it all—with your compassion for humanity still intact— then you don't even need to read *The Flower Ornament Scripture* and can walk on into the park and sit on a bench like Antoine Roquentin in Sartre's *Nausea* staring at the gnarly roots of a chestnut tree where they disappear into the earth and for each and every lack of meaning there will suddenly be a new word in a new language in which you are completely and totally fluent and something like gratitude will well up in your throat as sweet as the nectar going down the gullet of that red-and-green shimmering hummingbird hovering in mid-air over there by those bright pink flowers finely dusted with carbon particles from the diesel exhaust of the trains and buses and other rumbling traffic just on the other side of the ivy-covered wall which separates you from not a single other thing.

A POEM FOR RACONTEURS

In the blue-hazed seaman's mission
the TV is hotwired and pulsing.
In the blaze of the marquee outside
her fist opens slowly like a
fleshy pink five-petal flower
as though to separate
the real from the unreal.
On the downtrodden sidewalk
in front of the Star Hotel
the animal logic kicks in with a clunk.

Like the tricks of the light
in a forest that's not primeval
or in an alley that smells like piss—
where the dead and the undead
are vying for a conjured moment
of pure unadulterated visibility
in the possibility afforded by
the magnanimity of negative space—
he's making up his sea stories
and she's making up believing them.

BONJOUR, MONSIEUR SARTRE

People who love people who hate other people
often look up and see the woman in the moon.
They think that with the right cameras and mirrors
they might begin to discover who they really are,
perhaps understand the furtive semblance
toward which they cleave in their rented rooms
in the nouveau régime. People who love people
who hate Sartre might not know that he liked to dine
at Maître Albert, Les Marronniers, Le Balzar
and the Brasserie Demory. Only people who have
actually been there know that the
temperature of the sidewalk is only of significance
when your face is being shoved down against it
by some asshole in a black leather jacket
who thinks he knows the true meaning of freedom.

IDIOT SAVANT

In a courtyard of fading nobility
or in a factory lunchroom—
on a barstool or a rough-hewn pew
in the church of unraveling memory—
under a tree of knowledge
or in a shit-stinking barn—
you learn to yield to perfection
and to embrace contingency.

Eye to eye with an animal—
no language in common and yet
nothing is missing—
while the beasts hunt other beasts
in the light that shines at night.
From which moment on
do all other moments
suddenly become subordinate?

BEING AND NOTHINGNESS REDUX

The body awakens the mind.
The mind is like an X-ray of a bird;
the wings are so fragile and thin
that the X-rays pass through
the fan-like filigree of feathers
without registering an image,
so that only darkness appears.
That darkness is also a lightness,
the lightness that allows birds to fly.

The mind awakens the body.
The body is like an X-ray of a church;
the church is so brick-thick-solid
that the X-rays bounce back
and becloud the eyes of the viewer,
the same viewer who is trying to
unlearn the blinding difference
between darkness and lightness,
between being and its opposite.

A POEM FOR RAPTORS

A bank of clouds slips easterly in front of the sun muting all color lessening the contrasts and plunging the bird market into a huge vacuous silence in which only the squeaking door of a rusty birdcage flopping to and fro in the breeze can be heard like the creaking saloon doors in some surreal spaghetti Western providing an epiphanic aperture into which one might choose to delve for a fractured moment of relentless self-introspection and perhaps come up with something as seemingly apodictic as *there's always the possibility that I'm better off than I would be if I wasn't the way I am even if I have no idea how it is I got to be this way* and then the clouds go scudding off toward the strait and the harsh North African sunlight comes sweeping down the tiered cubist-looking hillside toward the harbor while the metallic blue-green of the peacocks and the bright yellow of the canaries and the predatory gaze of the falcons would like to dazzle my eyes but they're already locked on the glinting blades of the knives two loudly arguing bird merchants have pulled in order to settle their angry dispute in a manner not entirely uncommon in this part of the world.

OPEN-HEART BURGLARY

In the dusty postbellum antechamber of an old boatyard in Dithmarschen I brush the dust off a book and read how the ancient Chinese associated magpies with good luck and crows with bad luck and I look out the window and see four magpies harassing Billy the cat in the long green driveway wondering what became of the crows that used to live in the big poplars while I muster the necessary resolve for another wordless conversation with the weak and the strong while the peaches from Spain that smell like sun are languishing in the darkness of my German pantry just down the hall from where I'm weighing these truths and consequences and coming to such conclusions as the needs devise the ways and you go someplace to get something and return to from where you came and it's a very stubborn bird that rises up from the ashes.

THE CURVE

Going through that curve
day in day out
as though oblivious

to that place on the corner
that sells wheelchairs
trusses & crutches & such

to say nothing of those
who might eventually
need those things

going through that curve
day in day out
as though oblivious . . .

LIKE A HEROIC LANDSCAPE

THE MACHINERY was running at its absolute limit THE DICTATORS and THE DESPOTS were sitting down to lunch with their cronies and partners in crime THE SMOKE from the rubble and ruins turned the sky a dusky yellowish-brown THE BLOOD trickled in the gutters like a glistening red snake THE WOMEN held their cell phones in the palm of one hand while adjusting their Gucci sunglasses with the other hand THE MEN preened themselves impulsively by way of their reflections in the Ferrari salesroom windows THE BULLET CASINGS strewn along the sidewalk sparkled like something precious THE SOLDIERS were drinking and carrying on THE CHILDREN were fighting THE PRISONERS were singing THE PILOTS were striking THE PLUMBERS were plumbing THE BUTCHERS were butchering THE PIMPS were guzzling cognac THE TAXPAYERS were furious THE BANKS were being rescued while THE REFUGEES drowned THE VOICES grew silent, withdrew altogether, then became one with the wind swooshing through the trees THE TEMPERATURE was rising THE BATTERIES were empty THE GLACIERS were melting THE CURRENCY of reality was being recalibrated daily THE DECORUM for the most part went completely unheeded THE MEMORY of what could have been was destined to perish THE ABSENCE of presence was soon to be ubiquitous and final.

A POEM FOR DIALECTICIANS

Driving the roads and reading the signs neat green rows of cabbage and horseradish stretching to the coast of the cold North Sea seeing the huge refinery in Hemmingstedt glinting in the crooked light of December as bleak and desolate as Antonioni's *Red Desert*—miles and miles of piping and manifolds—clouds of vapor rising from the cooling towers—stacks topped with wavering flares of flame—for the weak of heart perhaps a demonic vision—for pale poets cruising the unnatural world a site of comprehension there at the confluence of the innerworld and the ultraworld where form trumps emptiness and emptiness trumps form in a perpetual cycle of realization where perception becomes a reason to be alive and a song to be sung in a key not yet found.

A POEM FOR RADIOS

John Wieners wakes up
mid-afternoon

tremulous walls
itching psyche

reaches over to
turn off the radio

to put an end to that
cacophony of voices

before getting down
first words of a poem

but the radio
hasn't been on

all day.

FLORESCENCE

Deep underground in subterranean Hamburg's
waxy artificial light—subway car windows
framing the beauties and the beasts.
I could choke up on the florescent enhancement
they bring to the crucible of quotidian being—
the intimate anonymity folding us from the many
into the one. The sameness and the difference
sliding back and forth day in day out until
it's all the same difference—
what the number was before it was a number;
what the word was before it was a word;
what the thought was before it was a thought—
taking it all the way back to the source.
A last mentation in the fading light of the station
as we lurch into the steel-wheel-screeching darkness.

NEITHER WAR NOR PEACE

You speak in proverbs but the lay of the land
has an idiom all its own.
You remember the snow and you remember the heat
and you searched for systems and you found them.
Things that happened "back then"
have a place of their own as well;
an old Strauss waltz on the radio in the kitchen—
sparrows cavorting in a hedgerow
in slanting winter sunlight—
the decadent elegance of candles burning
while the sun's still up.
Neither war nor peace nor flowering evil;
but a system nonetheless.

CALIFORNIA POEM

You wouldn't think of rain as being something frail but it gets that way out here in California where the white-tailed deer use their wet black noses to just nudge it out of the way so they can bend down gracefully and chew the stringy green strands of wiry Spanish moss lying strewn among the long tall redwoods with their collective animal abandon and ears constantly swiveling in fur-lined apprehension.

GREAT BALLS OF DOUBT

Walking away from the camera—
treading the fine line
between memory and its antipode—
past time passing by and that
two-part harmony
created by the ongoing discourse
between the living and the dead—
the vexing enigma of roses
blooming in the Hafenstrasse
in late December—
like some kind of prophetic
Teutonic oracle
speaking in tongues of color.
In order to be lied to
you mustn't know the truth
but the truth
is inside you whenever you lie.

RUE FÉROU

Paris streets underfoot,
cleaving to history,
someone else's memory
burned into my own.

Remaining alive
by staying attentive
to the immanence
of daily life.

Man Ray's old studio
in the rue Férou
now occupied by
someone named Roswitha,

or so it now says,
on the tiny nameplate
next to the brass doorknob,
polished and gleaming,

time's inexpiable code
cracking, fracturing into
the vowels and consonants
of the present moment.

SUNDAY MORNING COMING UP

Sunday morning coming up out of the subway in Berlin the last threadbare shreds of lucidity torn away from the streets not far from the Alexanderplatz—consciousness now being recalibrated by the parameters of a venomous hangover in which Russian vodka, Afghani hashish, fragmented memories of a bad Johnny Cash cover band and a lousy poetry reading are all playing major roles—the transcendencies now locked in a cruelly designed holding pattern, constantly consternating—beginning to understand the hapless ratios for the very first time this time around—then someone wants to peddle you something and someone else wants to take it away from you, like that lovely old whore over there with the garish make-up and that Helen of Troy haircut—they say she was around when Picasso painted *Guernica*.

THE CLEFT

Pick a number; any number. That's what time it is. Pick another number; any number. That's how old you are. Put your glass down on the bar of the Amphore in Hamburg and look out the window across the rain-lashed harbor at the ships and cranes and containers stacked along the quays like a rusty Great Wall of China. Take a deep breath and let out a sigh.

Pull up out of that maudlin wallowing. Shove all those aching thoughts out to some painless periphery. Get that psychic alchemy working that turns death and loss into a transience that transcends. Pick up your glass and swirl the contents thoughtfully with the polished stoicism that you've been perfecting as of late and pick another number; any number at all.

APRIL POEM

A new bottle of Baron Otard cognac;
the new reprint of Malcolm Lowry's
Selected Poems; three different cats
on three different windowsills
scrutinizing the spring dusk with
feline intensity. Uta on the couch
engrossed in her book about ants.
These things define you before you
even know who you are.
Nights without numbers,
days without names, the newsreel
of reality unrolling in the void;
who is it that keeps trying to be "me"?

BARDO KITCHEN CYCLE

My father seated
at the kitchen table
adrift in his dementia
just a few months
before his death.
I'm standing behind him
tying the bib around his neck
flashing on the fact that
sixty-some years ago
while I sat in my highchair
at the kitchen table
he stood behind me
doing the very same thing.
Fucked up that the loved ones
all have to go and even more so
the way they have to do it—
sweet though the way
what goes around
comes around and holds fast
like a mountaineer's rope
connecting all us
hapless drifters.

GODZILLA VS. RATIOCINATION

Riding the bullet train from Tokyo to Kyoto on the Tokaido Shinkansen line—Mount Fuji the only fixed point in this 285-kilometer-per-hour blur through which I am being efficiently hurled with my skull-hammering-beer-sake-plum-liqueur-kamikaze-hangover of Godzilla-like magnitudes.

I glance down at my ticket and flash fortuitously on Tokyo being an anagram of Kyoto—or is Kyoto an anagram of Tokyo? Or has the age-old causality-dilemma of the chicken versus the egg now become some kind of baffling Zen-koan feedback loop in the toxic slur of my thoughts?

I look up at resplendent Mount Fuji again, as though the answer, rising up like an ephemeral wisp of volcanic steam, might be waiting there with all its refulgent dispensation. And it is. Mind trying to make a mountain out of a handful of rice.

A VERY LONG TIME REVISITED

In the sultry kitchen or in the
chattering street or in some
secret domestic location
downtown uptown all around
the elements of space and time
seethe and conspire
and come together
just this side
of a congress of confusion
and suddenly become
a "reality" winsomely realized
while at the dusty crossroads
under gathering clouds
the queried drifter points
and the weary pilgrim looks
down along the way
not yet traveled
where even now
the last of the red-hot gewgaws
are sparkling and shining
in the artificial light
of the jaunty bazaar
there at the outskirts
of that thing called civilization.

A POEM FOR PATRIOTS

Brand new shiny unopened bottle
of Russian vodka on the kitchen table
next to invisible unknown
mystery cake from the baker hidden away
in vaguely surrealist brown paper wrapping
each with their own promising portent . . .

The squeak of the ironing board in the next room,
Joan Baez maiming a Dylan song in the background;
red, green, blue and yellow plastic Easter eggs
swinging in the breeze in the neighbors' trees;
the words—purblind yet mercurial—
can still only say what the words mean.

On TV between shots of suicide-bomber carnage
and discreet mini-camera shots of the underside of
the turned down cards of tournament poker players
I saw in a documentary how the American lotus
grows up out of the same mud and muck
as any other lotus in the world.

INTERZONE

The inveterate hipster rises
but does not shine
shuffles across the vermin-infested floor
of his seedy Tangier hotel room
littered with the pages
of what will become *Naked Lunch*
shaves his bony mug, combs his wispy hair
puts on his suit and hat
goes out and burns another pharmacist
with a bogus script for Eukodal
then heads down through the
crooked streets of the medina
to the harbor for his morning constitutional
which consists of rowing out into
the wide blue bay
where the fishermen are yet to tire of
the curious spectacle and always grateful
for a laugh.

THE AGE OF ENLIGHTENMENT

When I saw your ideas of the Sublime and the Beautiful on TV I knew it was over for good. The last time I saw you we were waiting in the greenroom, you handed me a blue drink, smiled with your yellow teeth and a red light went on. I thought *what if this was a dream* and it was a dream. I thought *what if this was real* and it was real. I tried to change the channel but the remote control was now a baby porcupine and my fingers were a bloody mess.

OUT BACK

Out back my eyes are all over that flat green northern German landscape illumined by an oblique morning sun casting down its clear crystalline light while immediacy's insistence has me inwardly mobile, moving toward some jewel-like center, some glowing matrix, some shimmering source of enlightenment which probably isn't even half as bright as the diamond-like dewdrop sparkling in that blade of grass right over there.

ULTRAMARINE

Prosperous in our ignorance,
ignorant in our prosperity,
the laws of nature
rain down upon us
in our stylish waxed cotton
designer raincoats.

The hottest summer on record
and we're cooling our drinks
with chunks of ice
broken off from the
polar ice cap as it floats by
the kitchen window.

A POEM FOR VESTIGES

The light in the house
and the light in the garden
and the darkness behind my eyes
conspire to build an image.

The words within words
and the words that turn
on other words
perform their lonely rituals
of circumlocution.

The perfect shadows
traced back
to the silhouettes
that formed them
are another one of light's
many unspoken allegories.

Grief like a guttering flame
burns
but unlike fire does not
devour
and yet the ashes are everywhere
strewn with their cold
celestial symmetry.

WATERHEAD

Summer downpour
on metal roof
beating out
apocalyptic tattoo—

Motörhead
blasting on the stereo
just barely
keeping up.

A POEM FOR MONOSODIUM GLUTAMATE

A lattice of nerves
stuck in a hayloft
or standing down
on an urbane corner
gazing at fluid traffic
and the light that is
gathered and reflected there
while contemplating the
fractured relevance of
some analeptic credo
limned insomnious
in moonlit hypertension—
the one which says that
seventy-five percent
of what you know
is like words in a mirror
only to be understood
with the help of
yet another mirror.

JOURNEY TO THE END OF THE MIND

There in the park where I played as a kid
I saw them painting the brown grass green.
Just us early risers and the burgeoning of the coming day—
the clustered clarity of it all impinging trenchantly
on my slowly developing take of things
so early in the morning.
Entering into commerce I saw those who were unable
doing the best they could—
compromised by issues which they'll never overcome
but loved nonetheless by someone somewhere—
and there was a twang in the rusty heartstrings.

Later in the darkness I saw something altogether
different—it looked like a searing flame but it was just
the flickering glow of a huge TV—the actualities dawning,
yawning; colored as they were with their
unsettling palette of tempered uncertainty.
Recollecting the future while anticipating the past
I set out to reconcile the paradoxes
only to end up somewhere else entirely
and undergo the heavyweight realization that the
paradoxes have long since—maybe even always—
been wholly reconciled.

OUT-THE-WINDOW POEMS

Out-the-window poems
happen when you've been
reading James Schuyler
and looking out the window
instead of writing poems.

The wide summer sky
fills up with dreams and
then with sparrows and
then you're wondering
what do sparrows dream?

COMPETITIVE DECADENCE

Between these meridians
where pastoral alchemy
is loosened
on tough afternoons

these attributes
of tension and release
relinquished as a favor
for drinks with cheap gin

where a river
becomes a border
and divides countries
although the land remains one

where without cuff links
and electricity
the hardest work
was always done by hand.

A POEM FOR ANTEDILUVIANS

The end of the record
the needle
scratching in the groove
the silence becoming louder—
who can remember that?

The years plus the years
inflected with their own passing;
the heart owns nothing
but maybe stakes
a claim or two.

With an eye to the weather
both external and internal
forsaking attitudes
for directions not taken—
swimming in a dewdrop of sin.

The currency of memory
counted out in dreams
which bounce back the light
once mirrored in
the charity of experience.

IN HEAVEN

I heard myself in heaven
saying the same things
I'd said on earth.
I heard myself in hell
saying the same things
I'd said in heaven.
I heard myself on earth
saying the same things
I'd said in heaven and in hell.
I heard myself saying
the same things over and over
as though they were of
no importance whatsoever.

SEPTEMBER SONG

The lucid September sunlight
casts down its oblique rays
into the lush blades of grass
which throw back the light
like flying sharp shards
of sparkling green glass into
the soft dark iris of my eyes
where photons and neurons
scramble to get the image
to the brain which assesses
and conjectures and then
lets it be known that it
knows all that already.

BARBARY COAST

Precocious, to be sure, the dispositions not yet sorted, but
even at seventeen, one should know better—bounding up
the stairs of Lyle Tuttle's Tattoo Parlor on Seventh Street
next to the Greyhound Terminal in San Francisco where
scrawny Allen Ginsberg once toiled in the baggage room—

From behind a measured grimace I watch Lyle himself jab a
crude skull & crossbones into the white unmarred flesh of
my teenage forearm, ink & blood running together as only
a poet could see it—the first of many gestures toward all
those who might take me for something that I'm not.

MAGPIE SONATA

The black and white of it all; ancient majestic oak trees blasted over in the storm—entire rows of birch and poplar knocked down flat across undulating country roads and fields. But the magpies' nest high in the ash tree is still there—and the magpies too—I hear them as I come up the driveway, reconciled by their presence—the diametrical opposition of their two-tone color scheme (with that iridescent shimmer of metallic cobalt blue), gracefully united in the complementary relationship that some munificent god might have given them—their clacking tempestuous chatter—one on one, back and forth, black and white— ringing in my ears like some avian Scarlatti sonata swiftly hacked out on a vintage Underwood typewriter.

DIALING IN THE VERITIES

The dispatches come winging in
edged like razors
lustrous with myth and mystery
against a campy background of
German expressionist-noir shadows
filched from the muse known as
Our Lady of the Woolworth's
where I sat as a kid in 1960s America
surrounded by Dick-Tracy-comic citizens
at the Edward Hopperesque lunch counter
eating a grilled cheese sandwich
with a few slices of limp dill pickle
and a cherry Coke that hurt my teeth
unaware of the many different gambits
and puzzling opening moves
that would be plied upon my person
by those who meant "good"
or something they considered as such
in all the years to come
unlearned in the nomenclature
of the "outside" and the "other"
be it Jack Spicer's or Arthur Rimbaud's
oblivious to all the crippling desires
and their attendant disappointments
that would eventually train my ears
to ruthlessly comb the ether for the
one true frequency
that slices through all the others.

THE ART OF VICTORY

A hot, smoggy day in LA.
Bukowski wheels out of the lot
at the Hollywood Park racetrack,
past rows of cars shimmering
in the brassy California sun.

Bukowski is ninety bucks ahead today.
He roars out onto the freeway,
slips over into the fast lane,
turns up the Mahler symphony,
lights a big black cigar.

For the time being, he is
beyond poetry, beyond women,
beyond the post office, back rent,
and that long war of attrition
we all know as Existence.

He grins sublimely, focused on the
hard, glittering diamond of Fortune,
like a Zen monk tuning in
to the true meaning of life,
which is essentially the same thing.

A POEM FOR HEROES

A lunatic in a bar. Four-star manna raining down.
Flickering images on a TV; wars that aren't news;
points along a line that was once a narrative
but now bends obliquely, eschews linearity,
cleaves closer to some wayward elliptical truth.

They set 'em up for the lunatic, soldierly and alone,
and he drinks with a hollow-eyed materialism
and a greed that once might have been gusto
in the fading light of an airborne division tattoo
and some God-given emblems of virulent dispute.

THE ANTONYM OF SERENDIPITY

The antonym of serendipity is what you find breathing in these streets; the slick shimmer of the cobblestones, a caustic wind roaring around some red-brick corner— mental delinquency and psychic discord and the quotidian melodrama forever requiring someone's presence in order to make it "real." Halfway across the parking lot the climate conquers your face. The café is crowded with ruddy-cheeked farmers' wives and the stench of what Sartre was talking about when he was talking about "bad faith"; the same old white-haired apologists nurturing imaginary vendettas and cultivating the wayward wisdom gleaned from faulty translations and sundered transmissions. At the flea market down by the harbor in view of the tankers and freighters and nuclear reactors something amazing just never happened—like all that which led up to what you were thinking about and all that which led away from it. Survival has a price and it's not just vigilance. The messenger devours the message but before a body can meet a mind something feline happens and the filigree shadows of the shattered decorum become the new coinage.

THE DESCENT OF THE BOHEMIANS

Avenues of emotion—epic streets—with walls windows doors vehicles begrimed with the slavish subjectivity you can only call your own—that wished-for chemical imbalance or blast of hormonal dysfunction you could never achieve by yourself—not a mandate of perception but a way of apprehending the world.

A shattered notebook—a mirror full of words—the consumer crematorium we call the metropolis the mall the madness where jackals and vultures meet to act out parts of some picaresque William Burroughs routine in the cryptographic crepuscular endgame until the flash-point of desire ignites the cool blue pilot flame of utter contentment.

THE SPECIALIST YEARS

Wake up look out
past the fractured dream-shards
see waters rippled—trees bowed—
ornate cornices of cumulus
blowing west to east—
walk into the waiting arms
of that which will decimate you—
past the last brown town
past the last green glade
past the last clever lyrics
and the ringing guitars—
where gravestones and urns
and other silent syntax
act like periods and paragraphs
and other full-stop caesura
in the long sentences
of the passing millennia—
where birth and destruction
and the days and the months
keep piling up and up—
on the head of a tarnished pin.

LEGACY

Kerouac's letters
under glass
in a posh gallery
out on Melrose Place.

A check made out
to the local liquor store;
one of the last things
he ever wrote.

TEXAS BAR TURNAROUND

First I was a subject, then I was an object, then I was the narrative that held the two together. Then they destroyed me, then they birthed me again, and there I was, sitting on a stool in the womb-like cobwebbed nautical ambience of the Texas Bar in Lisbon, just a bottle's throw from the harbor, knocking back cervejas and cognacs, not just as some dumb pub-crawling tourist but with a bona fide Merchant Mariner's Document with full Qualified Member of the Engine Department rating and wages to burn, a thirst to be slaked, and a bone to be picked with fate and foreordination, and yet fully prepared to receive the contraries allotted to my person with suitable dignity and magnanimous grace.

An ancient whore whose youthful beauty had not been totally annihilated by the ravages of time sidled up next to me on an adjacent barstool and we began right merrily to dissect the vicissitudes of love and money. Some KLM pilots and flight crew at the other end of the bar said I looked like Donald Sutherland and bought me a drink. I reciprocated the gesture and relapsed deep into my inner-mind and began to consider the Attributes—on the bad days you wished they had an end; on the good days you can never count them all; while in the interim you continue to excavate that gritty crevice between the Disguised and the Overt, a lullaby from Eros bombinating in your ear.

MEIN FUCKING KAMPF

Over by the big living room window, looking out into the garden, my wife, in an out-loud conversation with herself which I am obviously expected to overhear, is enumerating what her soul requires in order to be at peace with itself and right away I catch myself thinking about how glad I am that I don't have a soul and that even if I did it would have no choice but to be at peace with itself and since the Knausgaard book I'm trying to read is so dreadfully boring, tedious, and totally devoid of any significance literary or otherwise, my mind is already wandering ever further afield and I'm wondering to myself (not aloud) what old Hugh Hefner is up to right now, if he's getting his nut or just lounging around in his pajamas and bathrobe and jaunty captain's hat or maybe doing both at the same time or if perhaps his fading virility might be the perfect symbol for the waning powers of my own dwindling intellect and the losing battle between sanity and madness?

HEAVEN & EARTH AT WAR

Emily Dickinson—
barely out of the womb—
already the dark meanings
are closing in around her.

It isn't long before
she's firing back her own—
toward what she reckons
to be the source.

Heaven & earth at war—
Emily caught in the crossfire—
an existential sentinel
in a white cotton dress.

THE VAGARIES

Tangier, boulevard Mohammed-V,
walking back to the Hotel Lutetia
on a wet October evening.

Nervous gusts slicing in off the strait,
rain drumming against closed shutters . . .

Paul Bowles dead and buried in upstate New York,
William Burroughs dead and buried in Kansas,
Alfred Chester gone crazy and gone . . .

Mohammed Mrabet ensconced on his farm,
Madame Porte's Tea Room
closed down and boarded up . . .

This ghostliness is very real.
As real as shadows and light
and the loaded interstices in between.

The title of tonight's experiment is
"The Vagaries of Transience."

My thesis will be delivered tomorrow at noon
at the Caves of Hercules

where a white scorpion
waits trembling
under a shiny black rock.

BENEDICTION

Today's November sky
a grubby sheet of platinum
suspended much too low for comfort

The last dozen-or-so apples
bobbing rhythmically
in the wind-blown tree
soon to be stripped of its leaves

A season of the mind
which hyperventilates
—unflinching—
under the weight of its own desires

The crunch of history
from which we
constantly decamp

Washing the cat's dirty dishes
doesn't make you
King of the Monastery.

A POEM FOR THE REAR GUARD

Along about the time
freedom became a product
and war the currency
with which that product
could allegedly be purchased

the gypsies packed up their things
and hit the road
and the dust kicked up by their horses
slowly settled on the tables outside
the Café des Despotes

where this poem was found
scrawled on a wine-stained tablecloth
in the blood-red gloaming
of one of the very last
evenings on earth.

RUMORS OF A DIVINE WORLD

The romanticism I've been cultivating all morning long
abruptly fades as I step out of the subway car
ascend the escalator and see the flakes of dandruff
on the shoulders directly in front of me
now thinking of consciousness as a tangible thing
like something you could put your hand on or under or
around maybe even caress and at the top of the escalator
everyone reeling off in all different directions—
a Catherine wheel of human purpose and intention—
the deep-fried smell of McDonald's and the clatter of the
shipyards wafting in on the icy-cold wind
shearing up from the Hamburg harbor—

A peroxide-blonde prostitute in a mini-skirt, knee-high
fur-lined boots, red lipstick, with piercing blue eyes
looking for business looks right past me deep into the
urban landscape where a lie considers another lie and
wonders if together they might become the truth—
affording me the sensation of appearing in a picture of a
mirror without being reflected in it—of seeing through
an aperture ripped open by chance à la André Breton—
of reaching out through the carbon and the ether to
bring the past up into the present in order to proceed
on into the future only to arrive there and find
that the past has already begun again.

A POEM FOR LAWNMOWERS

You're totally engaged in the quirky appearance of the beaded raindrops on the chromed caging of the shopping carts outside the supermarket when "the wife" says something funny but the Gatling-gun synapses have fired again and your eyes are already buried in some scintillating physiognomy cutting across your field of vision.

Back at chez poet the grass almost knee-deep, the paint peeling off in palm-sized flakes, stereophonic snarl of Captain Beefheart churning out of the hi-fi speakers much too loud for comfort—on the upside it can no longer be so excruciatingly painful that everyone knows you're a reprobate apostate committed to idleness and rancorous unsuccess.

PRODIGAL SON

Walking down the street
the afflictions held at bay
uninflected just reeling
feeling more feminine
marvelous and tough
than anyone in sight.
What is it that's so
fetchingly Elizabethan
about all those flowers
bending in the wind?
It's me, the crypto-symbolist,
addressing the nascent day,
crashing through the roof
of the church of testosterone,
solidifying the moment
in the flux of history where
no acolyte can ever hope to go.
Crossing the intersection
my eyes are met by
those of the hearse driver
whose smile collides with me
in the zebra-striped crosswalk.

AFTER THE WAR

In the laundromat
next to the liquor store
I asked her what she was doing
after the war.
Her eyes were as lucid
as Madame Blavatsky's
but the similarity stopped there.
Some cars hissed by
in the rain outside.
The liquor store got held up.
The laundromat closed down
and the wars go on and on.

THE THIN LINE

The thin line of casualties
that runs across your face.
The masks in the streets
and the panic they allow.
I only came
to pine in your woods
and now I'm lost here,
a hardened artery in
your radial grid.
Your countenance rusts
in televised anguish.
The medicine and the poison
look so much alike in this light.

SELF-PORTRAIT IN AISLE SEVEN

Not a single day
without its arduous impiety

just something else
you have to work your way through

like a sudden loss of personality
or a ribald extension of character

or like anything else that smacks you
upside your fervid cognizance

while cruising down aisle seven
of the supermarket on a Friday afternoon.

A POEM FOR TYPEWRITERS

That bird twitching on that branch has a certain garden-variety neurosis, not unlike a woman I know, whose disenchanted eyes can take in a waiter or a waitress or a pair of snakeskin boots in a boutique window but not the byzantine arabesque of smoke from a freshly lit Camel curling up toward the fly-blown ceiling of the Western Union office, where I sit ensconced in my latest guise as a superhuman disgraced by my own pride, like a would-be warlord slumming in the varieties of nihilistic experience.

But no one can hear what it is I'm hearing by way of derangement and abandonment and washing up on some foreign shore—this morning's imbroglio already kicking in like shunting boxcars slamming in the darkness—the code of the road now just a hum in the old wires. Illusions of immanence, verbal hallucinations, and that voice coming up out of the typewriter—loud, clear, and vatic as hell—and the kids, yeah, the kids these days, they don't even know what a typewriter is.

PERVASION

Today I'm idiosyncratic,
tomorrow I'm heliocentric,
in between I'm feline, canine,
just plain insane.

The featureless features
come my way
by way of "mediation"
and infectious pixilation.

On the way to the supermarket
I'm wondering if the libido
can have a libido of its own.
On the way back home, I realize it can.

The long march of desire
bridled by temperamental trepidations,
rust in the bottom of the iron teapot,
sleet rasping at winter windows.

The battered psyche is trembling,
wants a way out, or maybe a way in.
The familiarities go flying by.
Outside the inside is wavering too.

INTERSTICE

Some fine tension
between the spheres
of form and formlessness
which overlap and create
an intermediate space
of neither/nor in which
the sublime becomes electric;
in which a soldier
browsing a used car lot
is more concerned with
the aesthetics of a contour
than the art of war.

THE TURNSTILES OF SIN

Think about the doors you swing open in front of you and the doors you swing shut behind you and all the rooms you cross to get from one to the other in the long arduous trek across time and space. Think about a player or a swordsman or a healing king—or just any other way of thinking. Think about the virgins and think about the gods, about the sins that are deadly and the sins that are not. Think about where you were before you were there where you thought you understood. In the kitchen, sagacious but skeptical, you pull where it says OPEN HERE but OPEN HERE breaks off in your fingers and the damn thing is still unopened.

WHAT RUNS THE GAME

The money exchanges hands
but the value of those hands
remains unchanged.
That image—if it is indeed an image—
is riding with me today,
a co-pilot of sorts,
so that when she opens her mouth
to speak of living things
and what comes out is dead—
dead as a pile of banknotes and coins—
a language in which only the poorest
would dare to speak—
my feet are still anchored
firmly on the ground,
although my pockmarked fealty
to the lesser truths may be signaling
the termination of my social contract
during the rise and fall of
these times we might have lived in
vaingloriously or otherwise.

THE WHITE CITY

A grainy sequence in uncertain light
somewhere down by the harbor
looking through a dirty hotel window
into a sullen overcast morning
seeing what is to be seen there;
murky silhouettes of freighters
and spidery cranes against
the colorless expanse of the Tagus River
in Lisbon, like some symbolist mock-up
of a neo-impressionist painting
done by a dilettante jailbird
with too much time on his hands
while above the white city
the sky is the same metallic tone
as the incipient blue hue
shimmering in the hair of the old ladies
sitting in the Café Nicola
where refracted light
and the Eagles' "Hotel California"
are rebounding off the mirrored walls
of the art deco interior
and the waiter is getting ready
to step outside and put another hex
on the filthy fucking pigeons.

SPLEEN MACHINE

There by the tank farm along the Kiel Canal the cashed-in chips of temptation reconfigured through a rain-streaked windshield framing rusty tankers lined up at the fueling docks, a unilateral narrative in which the things themselves are doing all the talking, the flipside of that narrative being the perpetual condition of possibility in which I am invariably the weakest of all eligible participants—swooning, ducking, never even touching the ground—the rabbit-punch-mule-kick of a strange but beautiful young woman's unexpected smile and smooth *Hello* in the fitness studio derailing the quotidian continuity—the disdainful sneer of a skinhead aimed my way while I'm walking up the hill to town—spawning bullet-riddled blood-spurting Charles Bronson Clint Eastwood slow-motion Sam Peckinpah fantasies of vengeance and retribution while the ghost of Gandhi is whispering in my ear to take it easy, not to get all pushed out of shape just because some punk's not liking the way my mojo is working—no reason to get pulled under in yet another riptide of enticement—and in the gray months that precede spring—there in the bathroom mirror each morning—is that a real existent or an actualized possibility?

IN MEMORY OF THE PRESENT

The way you live coincides
with something else
but you don't know what it is.

Like the way a stolen Chevrolet
has its own majestic way
of gliding through the night,

both hands gripping the wheel,
criminal flex of your wrists,
adolescent fever of

peer-group validation burning
beneath the pearled perspiration
on your moonstruck brow.

YES I DID

I saw a Japanese sky above Germany
yes I did just outside the window of my
melancholy Leonard Cohen kitchen
yes I did with stark black naked leafless
tree limbs juxtaposed as crooked zigzag
haiku brushstroke silhouettes against the
austere cold azure of a crisp winter morning
in frosty Schleswig-Holstein swirling with
Van Gogh moods and emotions and contrary
and anomalous and ambiguous as a minimalist
Richard Brautigan poem yes I really did.

HOUR OF THE WOLF

"The truth can only be recalled, never invented."
—Marilyn Monroe

In this Ingmar Bergman film better known as "my life,"
shot through and through with chintz and vapors,
spectral estrangement, loony symbolism and a dearth of
saving graces, there is a certain edginess, albeit rational
and circumscribed, like Rimbaud's deranged senses (in
the proper translation), as memory and amnesia engage in
another one of their tedious dialogues which invariably
end in unresolved dispute, while the full moon appears
locked between the bare branches of the ash tree outside
my window giving birth to the illusion that time is indeed
a mere concept and not an actual thing since things change
and if they didn't they wouldn't be things at all like the
stream out there in which the moon and the tree are now
reflected which is flowing oh-so-imperceptibly through the
muted darkness yet flowing nonetheless.

REALITY IS A FLAVOR

Reality is a flavor,
a bony allegory
caught between the teeth,
the continuous discourse
between life and death;

the bee's honey,
the sea's salt,
a sour lemon,
a bitter life . . .

Five thousand cracks
in the monastery wall
but the light has to be
just right
in order to see them all.

A KINK IN THE ARC

From optimistic augmenter to cynical subtracter in the time it takes to finish a glass of Tempranillo sitting outside the Café Engel just across from the Basilica St. Laurentius in the Friedrich-Ebert-Straße in Wuppertal as evening descends and the lights go on and suddenly it's just like that Van Gogh painting of the café at night at the Place du Forum in Arles.

Random staccato flashbacks merge into the internal narrative flow; of teething on after-hours coke parties and ugly scenes of the rites of manhood in redneck bar parking lots; of Paul Bowles pointing out his Tangier bedroom window talking about the wedding processions that pass by in the street below and the sounds of the drumming; of a strange woman in a strange place looking at me not knowing what to think and me looking back at her not knowing what to think.

The associations are made but not the connections. Like an unjust law or a cruel custom. The arc of perception bending all the way back around to the source; the lone perceiver, moored in that murky interstice between the condition and the cause, blindness incorporated into things you can't see anyway—your works in progress, your shadow in the mirror, your image reflected in a crystallized sun.

A POEM FOR STOPLIGHTS

The smell of death wafts westward from the slaughterhouse down by the river, drifts across the parking lot of the supermarket next door and hangs idly above an intersection where a livestock truck loaded with pigs is waiting for the stoplight to change.

The pigs are well-fed, chemically balanced, a little restless, and despite the noise and discomfort, somewhat curious as well. They raise their snouts and sniff the air, wet pink nostrils expanding and contracting, as the light finally turns green.

RITUALS OF IMPENITENCE

It was that time of day when
the length of a man's shadow
is the same as his height.
In the cemetery I saw a couple
walking and holding hands.
I glimpsed them through the trees
and felt like some kind of voyeur.
Behind a giant marble tombstone
I saw two rats fucking.
They looked right at me, through me,
and went on fucking.
I looked away, not wanting to be
reminded of any kind of anything.
I walked out of the cemetery and
into the park, where sunlight
could be seen glinting off of the
discarded needles and syringes.
The plan for the hijacking
of the vehicle to your heart
was almost interrupted
by the birds in the trees
who were not singing but rather
talking to me about avian theophanies
and "celebrity entropy" and
the night not conforming to the day.

IN THE RUE DE BABYLONE

The hour parting like a curtain
to reveal the naked infirmities.
The mirror scratched at with a fingernail
to find out who's living behind the glass.
The hotel room flushed with early morning light,
the Paris streets a carbon-spewing murmur
mumbling in the subsonic background.
The pages of age flipping back and forth
in the breeze fluffing in the open window.
The federation of sensations faltering
in the upsweep of the day's unfolding.

THE KEY

You know that each step will take you closer
to the end. You also know that each step
could bring you closer to the beginning.
You know this like the brittle truth that it is,
which you carry with you like a pocketed key
to some grim gray zoo in an abandoned city
behind enemy lines in which exotic fur,
panzer-like skin, and colorful feathers languish
behind cold steel bars, all ears tuned in
anticipation of the clicking of the rusty lock.

WAITING FOR THE VULGARIANS

The painter paints a poem in black & white.
The poet paints a fist full of flowers,
a cloud held aloft by angels, a syringe
loaded with bliss & one voluptuous bystander
bestowed with the innocence
of her own making, scanning the emptiness
across its breadth & depth while taking notes
for her own personal book of disquiet.
From here on out it's cluster versus manifold
& the slippery mercy of a harbor town
in thick January fog, analog to something
that runs in another direction,
drinking spirits & fingering toadstools
under a rain-thrumming tin roof,
a bowl of porridge & a nickel-plated revolver
on the kitchen table, the owl-skull ashtray
swarming with stale butts.

SUPERABUNDANCE

No it's not a big black shiny bird it's a white seabird with terrified eyes completely covered with sticky black fuel oil collapsed in a shivering heap on an oily beach turning its head to look directly into the camera as the photographer snaps a photo opening wide its once-yellow beak tilting its head back to let out a long harrowing scream which of course you can't hear in the temperate comfort of your winter-warm living room thousands of miles away where you look down at the photo in today's newspaper before you fold it up and throw it away with all the other papers in the recycling box like yesterday today and tomorrow.

THE WHEEL

They built my heart all wrong because it's like a box without apertures when it should be more like a wheel that turns for the road of love and loss and sorrow is a long and zigzagging one the navigation of which requires a supple mobility not to be found in right angles corners and flat surfaces and to compensate they made my brain in the image of a perfect gilded birdcage from which colorful songbirds once might have sung enraptured songs where instead they mistakenly installed a rusty hamster wheel which squeaks and squeaks day and night as the resident lemmings with flattened ears and sleeked-back whiskers run in vain searching for the next likely precipice from which to leap through the waiting air.

THE SKIN INSIDE

Out there past the last old windmill
and the last stagnant canal—
the no-man's land of western Dithmarschen—
cabbage and horseradish in rows of staggering accuracy
stretching all the way out to the frigid
gray-brown waters of the North Sea—
hard-hatted Day-Glo-vested workers perched high
in the new steel pylons rigging cables to connect
offshore wind parks with the anthills of civilization—
I've got one hand on the steering wheel,
the other on the dial cranking up King Tubby's
"A Better Version" nice and loud while waiting
most likely in vain in some kind of cerebral limbo
for the old symbolism to morph into
an entirely new vernacular—an idiom of sheer imagery
in which the images themselves have
no significance whatsoever but struggle nonetheless
to articulate the meaning of meaning—
a hall of mirrors where purity reigns
and the algorithm of death can no longer find you—
and if it's a truth to be realized that your body is not
your own, then it must be a delegated image of heaven,
while the skin inside has a luster all its own,
reflecting back the warm glow from within.

PARABELLUM

In July enough rain to get the stream
flowing in the other direction;
but sufficient sunlight to raise the heads
of drooping flowers seen through windows
unwashed in all these years,
set in walls from which the paint
is unfurling like the Dead Sea Scrolls.
In August a metallic blue-green dragonfly
hovering above fallen rose petals.
In September a tiger-striped dragonfly
helicoptering along the boxwood hedge.
In October the eyes feasting on the fiery yellows,
blood reds, and rusty ochres of the leaves
of more trees than one could ever count.
Magic is always black or white but autumn
is a splintered spectrum of colliding colors
no cubist could ever have imagined.
In November the mind roaming along corridors
of memory hung with images of transience
vested with the wily sort of grace only seen
backwards in a mirror. The acrid smell
of burning bridges in no way unpleasant.
The crackle of the automatic weapons
just more static in the lurid background.
One lung full of hate, the other full of love;
in one breath I can say everything
that needs to be said. Yesterday is legend,
today is allegory, tomorrow is myth.

THE MAN FROM MONTEREY

> "I would rather play 'Chiquita Banana' and have
> my swimming pool than play Bach and starve."
> —Xavier Cugat

In the "real" world,
which is sort of like
the "ideal" world
yet different—more like
a reverse parallel universe
in which reality resembles
a TV game show where
the watercolor paintings
of Adolf Hitler and the
poetry of Radovan Karadžić
are offered as prizes—
the muesli-eaters
are cowering at the edge
of the oasis caught
in the blinding headlights
of an idling Land Rover
and you're Xavier Cugat
you're married to Charo
your Chihuahua is smiling
and life is just terrific.

ODE ON REALITY

A white-walled room
with windows opening
onto a green garden

where a blackbird
roots diligently under
wet brown leaves.

Reality speaking to me
in accordance
with my understanding;

the human race
a puppet show
in the animal kingdom.

EQUIPOISE REDUX

Snow all day then
clouds breaking up at evening—

golden strip along horizon
where blazing orb of sun

is seen through arterial
tree-branch tentacles—

quivering coppery-orange light
and then it's gone.

I'm at the edge
but the edge is in the middle

between the edges of
knowing and unknowing.

CODA

You see a shape you
read a phrase you obey
a law you have a dream
which is very bewildering
yet makes no end of sense—
you walk the wavering line
between sign and enigma
the jittery tension between
what can and what cannot
what will and what will not
sending a crackling current
buzzing through the void—
wait a good long while
before you place that period
at the end of that sentence
thus sealing it up like
some dark musty tomb
or do you trust yourself
to put a caesura in the
middle of all that
momentariness?

MARK TERRILL (*right*) is a native Californian and former merchant seaman. He has lived in Germany since 1984, working by turns as a shipyard welder, a cook, for the post office, and as road manager for rock bands, all the while publishing numerous collections of poetry and prose, such as *Bread & Fish* (The Figures, 2002) and *Diamonds & Sapience* (Dark Style, 2017). His work has appeared in print and online in more than a thousand journals and anthologies, including *City Lights Review, Bombay Gin, Empty Mirror, Jacket, Diagram, Rattle, RHINO,* and *Talisman,* and been translated into French, German, and Portuguese. Terrill has also translated poetry by Jörg Fauser (*An Evening in Europe,* Toad Press) and Rolf Dieter Brinkmann (*An Unchanging Blue: Selected Poems 1962-75,* Parlor Press).

JON LANGFORD (*left*) is a musician and visual artist who lives in Chicago. Born in Newport, Wales, he first came to prominence with art/punk music collective the Mekons, who met at Leeds University in 1976 and have been performing together ever since; their most recent album is *Deserted* (2019). He has also released many recordings as a solo artist and with other bands (the Three Johns, the Waco Brothers, Four Lost Souls, and more). Langford's art has been collected in two books, *Nashville Radio* (2006) and *Skull Orchard Revisited* (2010). In 2015 he was the artist in residence at the Country Music Hall of Fame, which commissioned him to paint a series of portraits for its exhibition "Dylan, Cash, and the Nashville Cats: A New Music City." He is represented by Yard Dog Gallery in Austin, Texas.

CPSIA information can be obtained
at www.ICGtesting.com
Printed in the USA
JSHW020452050720
6480JS00001B/3